LUCY MICKLETHWAIT was born in Quetta, Pakistan, and brought up all over the world; her parents settled in Scotland. Together with Brigid Peppin she wrote the *Dictionary of British Book Illustrators: The 20th Century*, which won a Library Association Award in 1983. She is the author of the highly successful I Spy series, which includes *Numbers in Art, An Alphabet of Art, Transport in Art, Shapes in Art* and *Animals in Art*. Her other children's books include *A Child's Book of Art, Spot a Cat* and *Spot a Dog* (both winners of the Parents' Choice Award in 1995), *A Child's Book of Play in Art* and *Discover Great Paintings*. Other titles in the First Art Book series include *Animals: A First Art Book* and *Children: A First Art Book*. Lucy lives in East London.

For Walter and Molly

First published in Great Britain in 2005 by
Frances Lincoln Children's Books, 4 Torriano Mews,
Torriano Avenue, London NW5 2RZ
www.franceslincoln.com

This edition publishing in 2009 in the US

British Library Cataloguing in Publication Data available on request

ISBN 978-1-84507-933-8

Set in Stone Sans

Printed in China

1 3 5 7 9 8 6 4 2

Colors

A First Art Book

Lucy Micklethwait

F

FRANCES LINCOLN
CHILDREN'S BOOKS

Red

red cherries

red hat

Yellow

yellow sunflowers

yellow dress

Blue

blue sky

blue
sea

Orange

orange oranges

orange cars

Green

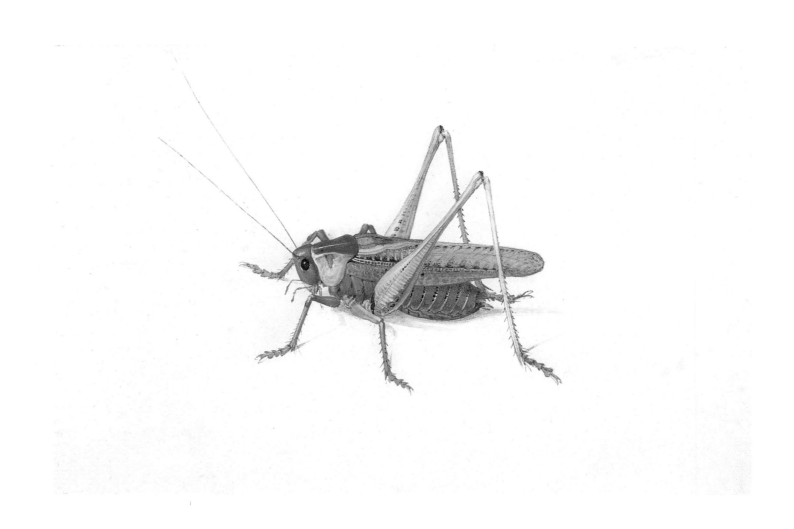

green grasshopper

green grapes

Purple

purple fox

purple mountain

Brown

brown books

brown owl

Pink

I LOVE YOU

Peter Blake

pink heart

pink chair

Black and White

white duck

black bat

Picture List

Red
red cherries
Still Life with Cherries and Carnations, Giovanna Garzoni
(1600–1670)
Watercolour on parchment
Palatina Gallery, Florence

red hat
Portrait of a Young Man Holding a Medallion of Cosimo I de Medici
(1475), Sandro Botticelli (1444/5–1510)
Tempera on wood
Uffizi Gallery, Florence

Yellow
yellow sunflowers
Bouquet of Sunflowers (1881), Claude Monet (1840–1926)
Oil on canvas
The Metropolitan Museum of Art, New York, Bequest of
Mrs H.O. Havemeyer, 1929

yellow dress
Three Sisters of the Copeland Family (1854), William Matthew Prior
(1806–1873)
Oil on canvas
Museum of Fine Arts, Boston, Bequest of Martha C. Karolik

Blue
blue sky
Vincent's House at Arles (1888), Vincent van Gogh (1853–1890)
Oil on canvas
Van Gogh Museum, Amsterdam

blue sea
View from Satta in Suruga Province from the series *Thirty-six views
of Mount Fuji* (1858), Ando Hiroshige (1797–1858)
Woodblock print
Ashmolean Museum, Oxford

Orange
orange oranges
Wrapped Oranges (1889), William J. McCloskey (1859–1941)
Oil on canvas
Amon Carter Museum, Fort Worth, Texas
Acquisition in memory of Katrine Deakins, Trustee, Amon Carter
Museum 1961–85

orange cars
2000 Horses and Turbo-powered (1972) from the series *Bunk*
Eduardo Paolozzi (born 1924)
Screenprint, lithograph and mixed media on paper support
Tate Gallery, London

Green
green grasshopper
Grasshopper, Maria Sibylla Merian (1647–1717)
Watercolour on paper
Courtauld Institute of Art Gallery, London

green grapes
White Grapes, James Sillett (1764–1840)
Watercolour on paper
Norwich Castle Museum and Art Gallery, Norfolk

Purple
purple fox
Fox (1911), Franz Marc (1880–1916)
Oil on canvas
Von der Heydt-Museum, Wuppertal

purple mountain
Goatfell, Isle of Arran (1993), Craigie Aitchison (born 1926)
Oil on canvas
Private collection

Brown
brown books
Bookshelves (c.1725), Giuseppe Maria Crespi (1665–1747)
Oil on canvas
Civico Museo Bibliografico Musicale, Bologna

brown owl
The Little Owl (1508), Albrecht Dürer (1471–1528)
Watercolour on paper
Albertina Gallery, Vienna

Pink
pink heart
I Love You (1982), Peter Blake (born 1932)
Hand-knotted rug
The Whitworth Art Gallery, Manchester

pink chair
Little Sweet (1944), William H. Johnson (1901–1970)
Oil on paperboard
Smithsonian American Art Museum, Washington DC

Black and white
white duck
The White Drake, Joseph Crawhall (1861–1913)
Watercolour and gouache on linen
National Gallery of Scotland, Edinburgh

black bat
Bat and Full Moon (early 1900s), Yoshikuni
Woodblock print
Private collection

PHOTOGRAPHIC ACKNOWLEDGEMENTS
red cherries: Galleria Palatina © photo Scala, Florence
red hat: Uffizi Gallery © photo Scala, Florence
yellow sunflowers: Metropolitan Museum of Art, New
York/www.bridgeman.co.uk
yellow dress: Museum of Fine Arts, Boston, Massachusetts/
www.bridgeman.co.uk
blue sky: Van Gogh Museum (Vincent van Gogh Foundation)
blue sea: Ashmolean Museum, University of Oxford/
www.bridgeman.co.uk
orange oranges: Amon Carter Museum, Fort Worth, Texas (1985.251)
orange cars: © Eduardo Paolozzi 2005. All rights reserved, DACS/photo
© Tate, London 2004
green grapes: © Norwich Castle Museum and Art Gallery
green grasshopper: Courtauld Institute of Art Gallery, London
purple fox: Von der Heydt-Museum, Wuppertal/
www.bridgeman.co.uk
purple mountain: © courtesy of the artist/www.bridgeman.co.uk/
photo Grahame Jackson
brown books: Civico Museo Bibliografico Musicale, Bologna/
www.bridgeman.co.uk
brown owl: akg-images/Erich Lessing
pink heart: © Peter Blake 2005. All Rights Reserved, DACS/photo
The Whitworth Art Gallery
pink chair: Smithsonian American Art Museum, Washington DC
© photo Scala, Florence
white duck: Private collection/www.bridgeman.co.uk
black bat: Private collection

OTHER TITLES BY LUCY MICKLETHWAIT
FROM FRANCES LINCOLN CHILDREN'S BOOKS

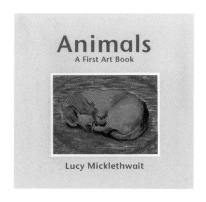

ANIMALS: A FIRST ART BOOK

Here are 18 exciting works of art featuring a range of animals,
from spotty to feathery, and creepy crawly to cuddly.
The artists, chosen from five centuries of art around the world,
include Dürer, Stubbs, Hokusai, Renoir, Warhol and Hockney.
A perfect introduction to art for the very young.

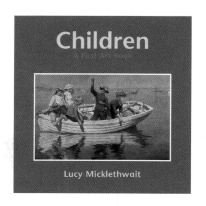

CHILDREN: A FIRST ART BOOK

Eating ice-cream! Playing a tune! Fishing in the sea!
Here are 18 unique works of art chosen to illustrate all kinds
of activities in a child's day – boys eating by Murillo,
a child writing by Renoir, a girl sleeping by Millais...
Lots to look at, lots to talk about.
A perfect introduction to great art!

Frances Lincoln titles are available from all good bookshops.
You can also buy books and find out more about your favorite titles,
authors and illustrators on our website: www.franceslincoln.com